MW01616112

A Life Dear to God

Deron J. Biles

Copyright 2025

ISBN: 978-1-953606-22-8

Published by Engedi Publishing LLC Sunrise Beach, Texas

Dedication

To our amazing family at Sunnyvale First Baptist Church with whom I am honored and grateful to serve

Acknowledgments

There are many people who have contributed to this book. I am grateful to Andy Spencer and the Engedi Group for helping to make this book possible.

I am very thankful to Jan Modisette for editing my work. If I used the comma appropriately in this work, it's probably due to her.

I am thankful to Jill Rawls for her amazing assistance in virtually every area of my ministry and especially for her encouragement in this work.

I am grateful to Ronnie Bilbrey. His encouragement and assistance in this book has been invaluable. He exemplifies everything I was trying to express about a faithful Disciple-maker.

I am grateful for Brian James and Taylor Curry for their assistance with the cover design for the book.

CONTENTS

A LIFE DEAR TO GOD

Introduction

A Life Dear to God is a 40-day devotional journey drawn from the life and ministry of Timothy. The plan is divided into 8 weeks, five days a week. It is designed as a supplement for one's regular, personal Bible study and is intended to move a believer from the early stages of faith to maturity in Christ.

Timothy's name means "beloved" or "dear to God."

From the study of Timothy's life, believers can learn lessons on faithfulness, service, and character that will apply to every area of their spiritual lives.

Paul's Ministry Companions

The Apostle Paul had many co-workers throughout his ministry. He often included names in his letters to recognize their work and affirm them in their ministries. Some of those worked with Paul in churches, and some traveled with him on his missionary journeys.

One of the first companions of Paul was Barnabas. Barnabas was exemplary in every respect. He is a model of generosity towards the church in Jerusalem (Acts 4); he was key in Saul being welcomed into the church; he was a teacher in the church in Antioch; and he recruited Saul for his first missionary journey. He was also later commissioned with Saul (then called Paul) as a missionary sent out by the community in Antioch.

Barnabas was an equal partner to Paul, the "Zeus" to his "Hermes," until they split after the first missionary journey. Their division occurred because of a dispute between them regarding whether to include John Mark on the second journey, after John Mark's earlier desertion during the first missionary journey. Barnabas' willingness to give John Mark a second chance is commendable, even if Paul's objections are also understandable. Though the two apostles go their separate ways, I argue that their conflict arose out of a legitimate disagreement. Moreover, God used their separation to double the missionary force of the church, as Barnabas took Mark and went to Africa, and Paul took Silas and returned to the churches in Asia

Minor. Scripture does not say if there was further contact between them or if reconciliation occurred.

John Mark features prominently at the beginning and end of Paul's ministry. We meet John Mark in Acts 12. He was the son of Mary. The church met in her home. That was the place where Peter came when he was miraculously released from prison.

Mark joined Paul and Barnabas on the first missionary journey but left early in the journey (Acts 13:13). While it is not clear if Barnabas and Paul reconciled, clearly Paul and Mark did. In fact, near the end of his life, the person Paul seemed to want to see most was Mark. Paul described him as useful (2 Timothy 4:12).

After Paul and Barnabas parted ways, Paul worked closely with Silas. Paul and Silas began their journey together in Acts 15 at the Jerusalem Council. Silas was one of two messengers from the church in Jerusalem who were sent back to the church in Antioch in Acts 15:22, 27 along with Paul and Barnabas. The Jerusalem Council was the occasion when early church leaders met to discuss the theological question of whether Gentiles could receive the Gospel without first converting to Judaism. The presentation was made before the leaders of the church in Jerusalem that the Holy Spirit was working in the lives of Gentiles, and, upon hearing that, the Jewish believers rejoiced. Paul and Silas later traveled and served together in Derbe, Lystra, Philippi, Thessalonica, Berea, Athens, and Corinth. They were also imprisoned together in Philippi. Silas, also known as Silvanus, assisted Paul in writing the letters of 1 and 2 Thessalonians and seems to have worked together with Peter in the writing of the letter of 1 Peter (1 Peter 5:12).

Paul also served with Titus. Where Paul sent Timothy to Ephesus, he sent Titus to Crete. In Titus 1:5, Paul gave Titus instructions to set in order what was lacking in Crete and appoint leaders in the church. Like he did with Timothy, Paul called Titus "my son" in Titus 1:4.

Titus was Greek (Galatians 2:3). He had probably become a Christian under the influence of Paul and had become one of the apostle's protégés (Titus 1:4). Titus had been with Paul since the apostle's early ministry. He accompanied Paul and Barnabas on their mission to the Jerusalem church when Paul was laboring in Antioch of Syria, Titus' home.

Paul's relationship with Titus began very early in his ministry. In Galatians 2:1, Paul, Barnabas, and Titus came to Jerusalem 14 years after Paul's conversion. This was before Paul's first missionary journey.

Titus does not appear in Acts; in fact, he does not appear until Galatians 2:1-3. We later see him in 2

Corinthians 2:13; 7:6, 13, 14; 8:6, 16, 23; 12:18. In 2 Corinthians 8:23, Titus is described as a partner and fellow worker.

Titus was also Paul's special representative to the Corinthian church during Paul's third missionary journey. He carried the "severe letter" from Ephesus (2 Corinthians 12:18; cf. 2 Corinthians 2:3-4; 7:8-12) and met Paul in Macedonia (2 Corinthians 7:6-16). He was, in addition, the leader of the group of men Paul sent to the churches in Macedonia and Achaia to pick up the collection for the poor saints in Jerusalem (2 Corinthians 8:6, 16, 23). Paul also requested Titus to come to Nicopolis (Titus 3:12) and sent him to Dalmatia (2 Timothy 4:10). Tradition suggests that Titus eventually became the first bishop of Crete and died there in advanced years.

Luke seems to have joined Paul early in his second missionary journey (Acts 16:10). He was Paul's friend, physician, and traveling companion. He was also an early church historian and Scripture writer. Luke wrote the New Testament books of Luke and Acts. Some believe he also wrote the book of Hebrews.

Paul led Lydia and her household to the Lord in Philippi (Acts 16:14). She invited Paul to stay with them and worked with Paul in making and selling purple cloth. Lydia is often seen as the first European convert in Paul's ministry.

Aquila and Priscilla were a faithful couple Paul met in Corinth on his second missionary journey (Acts 18:1-2). Aquila and Priscilla were prominent in Paul's travels (Acts 18:2-3, 18-19, 26; Romans 16:3-5; 1 Corinthians 16:19; 2 Timothy 4:19). Paul referred to them as his "co-workers" (Romans 16:3–4) and twice mentions churches that met in their home (Romans 16:5; 1 Corinthians 16:19).

Another worker with Paul was Apollos. Paul met Apollos in Ephesus (Acts 18:24-28). Apollos was described as eloquent, competent in Scripture, and one who vigorously refuted the Jews. He was mentored by Aquila and Priscilla, who "taught him the way more accurately" (Acts 18:26), after which he "powerfully refuted the Jews" (Acts 18:28). He later served faithfully in Corinth (Acts 19:1).

We don't know much about Paul's companion named Erastus. He was sent along with Timothy ahead of him to Macedonia. Erastus, along with Timothy, "assisted Paul" (Acts 19:22).

Aristarchus was another of Paul's traveling com-panions. He is mentioned five times in the New Testament (Acts 19:29; 20:4; 27:2; Colossians 4:10;

Philemon 24). Each time Aristarchus is mentioned, he is described as being "with" Paul. He traveled with Paul (Acts 19:29), accompanied him (Acts 20:4), and even was arrested with him (Colossians 4:10; Philemon 24).

Another man who served with Paul was Gaius. Gaius is mentioned in Acts 19:29; 20:4; Romans 16:23; 1 Corinthians 1:14; and 3 John 1. Paul described him as a "host to me and to the whole church" (Romans 16:23). Perhaps only in eternity will we fully appreciate the impact of his hospitality.

Another of Paul's companions was Trophimus (Acts 20:4; 21:29; 2 Timothy 4:20). He was from Asia. Paul specifically mentioned in 2 Timothy 4:20 that he left Trophimus sick in Miletus, which emphasized the urgency for his appeal to Timothy to come quickly.

Tychicus is mentioned in Acts 20:4; Colossians 4:7-9; and Ephesians 6:20-21. Paul described him as *"a beloved brother, faithful minister, and fellow servant in the Lord"* (Colossians 4:7). Paul sent him to Colossae with Onesimus. Paul also depended on Tychicus to minister to the church in Ephesus (Ephesians 6:21).

Paul mentioned a companion named Justus (he is also called Jesus) once in Colossians 4:11, where he described him as among the circumcised (meaning he was

Jewish), a *"co- worker"* for the kingdom of God, and a comfort to Paul. Nothing more is known about him.

Paul mentioned Epaphras three times in his letters. Each time, he included a description of him. In Colossians 1:7, he described him as a *"fellow servant,"* in Colossians 4:12, as *"a bondservant of Christ,"* and in Philemon 23, as his *"fellow prisoner."* In addition, in Colossians 4:12, Paul added that he always labored fervently on behalf of the believers in Colossae in prayer, pleading with God that they would stand "perfect and complete in all the will of God."

Moreover, he seems to have been with Paul when the Apostle wrote the letter to the church in Colossae (since he ministered to them; cf. Colossians 1:7 & 4:12) and was apparently imprisoned with Paul when he wrote the letter of Philemon.

Another of Paul's companions was Demas. Demas was an intriguing character in Scripture. He is mentioned three times in Scripture: Colossians 4:14, Philemon 24, and 2 Timothy 4:10. In the first passage, he sent the church greetings along with Paul. In the second passage, he is described as one of Paul's fellow laborers. However, in the final passage, Paul notes that

Demas had forsaken him. The explanation made for Demas' departure is because he *"loved this present world."* That does not necessarily mean that he left his faith, but that he preferred the comforts of the world to the difficulties of traveling (and suffering) with Paul. Nevertheless, Paul took his departure personally *("he has forsaken me").*

Paul gave special attention to his companion, Onesimus. He is mentioned twice in Scripture in Colossians 4:9 and Philemon 10. To the church in Colossae, Paul described him as faithful and beloved. He was also someone Paul relied on to make known to them the things that were happening to Paul. In the letter to the church in Philemon, we learn more about Onesimus. He, at one time, was a slave of Philemon.

For reasons we are not told, he ran away from Philemon and apparently met Paul in Rome, who led him to faith in Christ. The letter of Philemon is Paul's appeal to Philemon on behalf of Onesimus, whom Paul was sending back to reconcile with his former master. In that letter, Paul described Onesimus (using a play on his name) as *"useful"* to him. Many have speculated, based on the writing of Ignatius (his letter to Ephesus), that Onesimus later became the bishop of Ephesus.

These were not all of Paul's companions. In addition to these, Paul mentioned 29 people in Romans 16 (two of whom, Aquila and Priscilla, have been discussed above), many of whom are praised for the work with him. Their names are Phoebe, Epaenetus, Mary,

Andronicus, Junia, Ampliatus, Urbanus, Stachys, Apelles, the household of Aristobulus, Herodion, the household of Narcissus, Tryphaena, Tryphosa, Persis, Rufus, Rufus' mother (whom Paul described as a *"mother"* to him), Asyncritus, Phlegon, Hermes, Patrobas, Hermas, Philologus, and Julia, Nereus, Nereus' sister, and Olympas. Most of these are only mentioned here in Scripture, but their impact on Paul's life was important enough for him to record by name.

There were times in Paul's ministry when he felt alone (Acts 17:14-16, 2 Corinthians 2:13; 2 Timothy 1:15; 4:9-12; Titus 3:12). But the more we read his letters, the more we realize the army of people God brought around him at pivotal times in his life.

A Study in the Life of Timothy

It is clear that Paul was blessed by many close associates and co-workers. But Paul's closest associate seems to have been Timothy. Not only did he address two letters to him, but he also listed him as co-author in six others (2 Corinthians 1:1; Philippians 1:1; Colossians 1:1; 1 Thessalonians 1:1; 2 Thessalonians 1:1; Philemon 1). Timothy was also with Paul in the writing of Romans (Romans 16:21).

Timothy joined Paul on the second missionary journey when the Apostle's evangelistic team traveled to Lystra (Acts 16:1-3). On Paul's second missionary journey, Timothy helped Paul in Troas, Philippi, Berea, Thessalonica, Athens, and Corinth. During the third missionary journey, Timothy was with Paul in Ephesus. From there Paul sent him to Macedonia (Acts 19:22). Later Timothy served with Paul in Macedonia (2 Corinthians 1:1, 19) and apparently traveled with the Apostle to Corinth (Romans 16:21). On the return trip to Ephesus, Timothy accompanied Paul through Macedonia as far as Troas (Acts 20:3-6). Still later, Timothy was with Paul in Rome (Colossians 1:1; Philemon 1; Philippians 1:1), and from there he probably made a trip to Philippi (Philippians 2:19-23).

Paul referred to Timothy as *"my son"* (1 Timothy 1:2, 18; 2 Timothy 1:2; 2:1), *"our brother* (2 Corinthians 1:1; Colossians 1:1; 1 Thessalonians 3:2; Hebrews 13:23), *"well-spoken of"* (Acts 16:1), *"a bond servant of Christ Jesus"* (Philippians 1:1), and one who *"does the work of the Lord as I do* (1 Corinthians 16:10). *Paul said of Timothy in* Philippians 2:20, *I have no one else like Timothy who will genuinely care for your welfare."*

Tradition says that Timothy died in Ephesus as a martyr. If that is so, that would mean that he kept Paul's advice in (1 Timothy 1:3) to remain in Ephesus.

Paul includes many descriptions and instructions for Timothy. Moreover, since we know something of Timothy's early life as well as his later ministry, we can trace a maturity in his Christian life that serves as a model for believers today.

This study will focus on the attributes of Timothy as described by Paul. We will see Timothy as a believer, a man of godly character, overcomer, co-laborer, encourager, friend, disciple, student, and pastor. From these, this study will focus on lessons we learn from him that apply to the lives of all believers.

If you are a new believer, just beginning your journey of faith, this guide is for you. The study will outline eight steps that may serve as guideposts for your journey of faith.

For others who have been walking with the Lord for some time, this guide is also for you. Like Paul (Philippians 3:12–15), none of us are there yet. We are instructed to keep making progress towards the goal our Lord has for us. Along the way, there are some things in the past we may need to forget and some things ahead towards which we must pursue. All the while, we keep our eyes focused on the "upward call of God in Christ Jesus."

This study will focus on eight steps of discipleship drawn from the example of Timothy and the encouragement of Paul in his life. These steps begin with the first steps of a new believer in Christ and progress towards the goal for all believers to develop into a mature disciple-maker. They are benchmarks of a maturing discipleship of Jesus Christ. The benchmarks we will examine and prayerfully pursue are:

1. Knowing Christ
2. Becoming More like Christ
3. Standing for Christ
4. Serving Christ
5. On Mission with Christ
6. Encourage Others in Christ
7. Maturing in Christ
8. Disciple Others to Know Christ and Grow in Him

A LIFE DEAR TO GOD

Week One

Know Christ!

This week we are going to examine the first benchmark of the Christian life. It is a genuine personal relationship with Jesus Christ. The most important decision that you will ever make is the decision to trust Jesus Christ with your life.

In this first week of our discipleship study, we are going to be challenged by a description of Timothy's personal relationship with the Lord, his commitment to grow in his faith, and the recognition of God's work in his life.

Timothy first learned faith at home. But Timothy was not a genuine believer because of his mother's or his grandmother's faith. There came a time when he made a personal commitment of his life to Jesus Christ. This is where discipleship begins.

This week is a study of Timothy's faith story, but it is also an examination of yours. If you do not know Christ or are unsure of your faith story, I encourage you to check out this link (www.sunnyvalefbc.com/youneverknow) to find out how you can know Him.

Day One

Read: 2 Timothy 1:5

"For I am mindful of the sincere faith within you, which first dwelled in your grandmother Lois and your mother Eunice, and I am sure that it is in you as well."

Learn: Timothy learned faith from his mother and grandmother but developed a genuine personal faith in Jesus Christ.

From this passage, we learn of Timothy's genuine faith. Timothy had a heritage of faith.

I'm grateful for a heritage of faith in my own life. As we will see, Timothy's background wasn't exactly a perfect tradition of faith. From Acts 16:1, we learn that Timothy's father was Greek and apparently was not a believer. So, Timothy had a racially and religiously mixed background.

Nevertheless, Paul said of Timothy, I am reminded of the genuine faith that is in you. Neither Paul nor Luke recount Timothy's conversion story. Instead, Paul recognized that Timothy's mother and grandmother had a profound impact on him. Timothy was a third-generation believer!

What would genuine faith look like in you?

Paul recognized Timothy for his *"genuine"* faith. The word Paul used to describe his faith literally means *"unhypocritical."* He may have been influenced by Mom and Grandma, but the genuineness of his faith was a testimony to the grace of God in his life and his faithful devotion to God.

Apply: *What is your faith story?*

If you believe in Jesus, you have a faith story.

Has there been a time when you professed genuine faith in Jesus Christ? _____. If not, I encourage you to study the Scriptures and the link above to learn about God's sacrificial love for you in Christ and how you can be in a relationship with Him.

Write out your faith story. How did you come to faith? Who were the people God used to bring you to faith?

_____

_____

_____

_____

_____

_____

_____

What does genuine faith mean to you?

_____

_____

_____

_____

_____

_____

_____

Day Two

Read: Acts 16:1-5

"Now Paul also came to Derbe and to Lystra. And a disciple was there, named Timothy, the son of a Jewish woman who was a believer, but his father was a Greek, and he was well spoken of by the brothers and sisters who were in Lystra and Iconium. ³ Paul wanted this man to leave with him, and he took him and circumcised him because of the Jews who were in those parts, for they all knew that his father was a Greek. ⁴ Now while they were passing through the cities, they were delivering the ordinances for them to follow, which had been determined by the apostles and elders in Jerusalem. ⁵ So the churches were being strengthened in the faith and were increasing in number daily."

Learn: In Acts 16:1, Luke described Timothy as a *"Disciple."* That suggests someone who is growing in his or her faith.

It is not entirely clear at what point in his life Timothy came to know the Lord. Acts 14:6 states that Paul went to Derbe and Lystra and preached the Gospel there. From that, some have argued that Paul led Timothy to faith in Christ on that first missionary journey.

However, in 2 Timothy 3:15, Paul admonished Timothy regarding *"the things you learned from childhood."* That would suggest that Timothy was reared in a home where he learned about faith (likely from his mother and grandmother).

Regardless of when he first came to faith, it is clear that Timothy was growing in it. One of the ways that God used to grow Timothy into a disciple was the godly influence of other people. Yesterday, we looked at how the Lord used Timothy's mother and grandmother to influence his faith. God also used Paul in his life. *Who has God brought into your life to bring about spiritual growth?*

Mr. Rogers used to ask children the question, *"Who are the people in your neighborhood?"* I want you to stop and think about the *neighbors* God has brought into your path along your journey of faith. Stop and give thanks to the Lord for the kindness of the Lord and for their impact on your life and journey of faith.

Now, in the same way that God has brought people into your life, God will use you to impact the lives of others. Acts 16:2 says that the *"brothers"* spoke well of Timothy. Clearly, he had an impact on them.

As we will see later in this study, not only did God use Paul in Timothy's life, He also used Timothy in Paul's life. Consider the timeliness of Paul's encounter with Timothy. Mark left during Paul's first missionary journey. Barnabas and Paul split. So, Paul and Timothy needed each other.

Apply:

What evidence is there in your life that you are growing in your personal relationship with God?

_____

_____

_____

_____

_____

_____

Who has God brought into your life?

_____

_____

_____

_____

_____

_____

_____

Into whose life has God brought you?

_____

_____

_____

_____

_____

_____

_____

Day Three

Read: 1 Timothy 1:18

"This command I entrust to you, Timothy, my son, in accordance with the prophecies previously made concerning you, that by them you fight the good fight."

Learn: God had a plan for Timothy's life long before he knew it.

The Bible teaches that God has a plan for your life (Psalm 138:8; Proverbs 3:5-6; 19:21; Jeremiah 29:11; Philippians 2:13).

Like Jeremiah (Jeremiah 1:4–10), God began working out His plan for Timothy's life before Timothy was aware of it. God may have been speaking about Timothy before he even came to faith. What an amazing thought that God knew about Timothy's life and ministry long before it happened.

Interestingly, this verse affirms that God inspired someone (we don't know who) to utter a prophecy related to Timothy. In fact, vs. 18 declares that "prophecies" (plural) had been made about Timothy.

It is not clear how Paul became aware of the "prophecies" related to Timothy. Perhaps believers told Paul of them upon Paul's selection of Timothy to affirm Paul in his choice.

Either way, these prophecies affirm Paul's confidence in Timothy as his partner as well as the church's affirmation of him. Paul saw God at work in and through Timothy even before Paul chose him. He was encouraging Timothy not to forget that God knew all along how He would use Timothy.

Apply:

What has God been doing in your life?

_____

_____

_____

_____

_____

_____

Do you know the plan God has for your life?

_____

_____

_____

_____

_____

_____

_____

Day Four

Read: 1 Timothy 4:14

"Do not neglect the spiritual gift within you, which was granted to you through words of prophecy with the laying on of hands by the council of elders."

Learn: This verse highlights the gift of God given to Timothy.

In this passage, Paul affirmed that God was doing something in Timothy's life. It's as though Paul was saying to Timothy, *"I see evidence of God's work in your life."* Has anyone ever said that about you?

Paul later exhorted Timothy in 2 Timothy 1:6-7 to "Fan into a flame the gift of God in you." *Those gifts were evidenced by Paul and the church.*

The Bible affirms in 1 Peter 4:10 that we all have at least one spiritual gift. That means that God has uniquely gifted you for the specific purpose He has for your life.

How has God been preparing you?

Apply:

From the list of Spiritual Gifts mentioned in Romans 12:4-8, what do you believe is your Spiritual Gift?

_____

_____

_____

_____

_____

_____

_____

Have others recognized those gifts in you?

_____

_____

_____

_____

_____

_____

_____

How can God use you in ministry?

_____

_____

_____

_____

_____

_____

_____

Day Five

Read: 2 Timothy 3:14-15

"You, however, continue in the things you have learned and become convinced of, knowing from whom you have learned them,[15] *and that from childhood you have known the sacred writings which are able to give you the wisdom that leads to salvation through faith which is in Christ Jesus."*

Learn: In this passage, Paul encouraged Timothy to "continue" in his faith.

The book of 2 Timothy contains a series of imperatives from Paul to Timothy. In this passage, Paul instructed Timothy to continue in the things he had learned and become convinced of. Paul must have been talking about those truths he learned from childhood, perhaps sitting at the feet of his mother and grandmother. The obvious implication was that Timothy was already engaged in God's plan for his life. Paul was encouraging him to stay at it.

We've already seen that Paul affirmed what God was doing in Timothy's life. In this passage, Paul encouraged Timothy to keep doing what he had been doing.

So, whatever lessons of faith Timothy learned from his mother and grandmother, they became the basis for his spiritual growth. In truth, you and I never grow past elementary spiritual things; we grow deeper in them.

To be sure, this affirms the investment of Scripture in a child's life. This is a responsibility parents have. It is also an opportunity Sunday School teachers, VBS teachers, or Kids Beach Club teachers have. You and I may never know the impact our encouragement in the life of a child will have.

Luke wrote that he wanted his readers to "*know* the certainty of the things you have been taught" (Luke 1:4). What do you need to keep doing in your walk with the Lord?

Apply:

How has God been working in your life?

_____

_____

_____

_____

What are you doing to keep growing; to continue in
what you have learned?

_____

_____

_____

_____

_____

_____

_____

Week Two

Prove it!

The second benchmark of the Christian life is becoming more like Christ. The origin of the term *"Christian"* refers to those who resembled Christ. It's not clear, in Acts 11:26, if the term was meant in a complimentary or derogatory way. Either way, the believers adopted the term as an identifying description of themselves and it is still used today.

Once a person commits his or her life to Jesus Christ, a process of spiritual growth should begin. As we spend time with Him through His Word and in prayer and by worshiping Him corporately with God's people, we will become more and more like Him. Paul said in Romans 8:29 that God has predestined believers to be conformed to the image of His Son.

Paul acknowledged that process in his own life (Galatians 2:19-20). When we have been crucified with Christ, He lives in and through us. That was Paul's admonition to the believers in Rome (Romans 12:1-2). John called it walking the same way He walked (1 John 2:6).

This week we are going to look at a change in Timothy's life, character, and decisions because of his faith in Christ. This becomes our second benchmark of a growing relationship with Christ—when our lives begin to look more like the One to whom we have pledged our lives.

Becoming like Christ ought to change our minds, our relationships, our priorities, and our conversations. In other words, how we talk and how we walk will reflect a life that is becoming more like Christ. It's a process. But we take hope in the comfort Paul expressed to the believers in Philippi that God will complete the work He started in you (Philippians 1:6).

Day One

Read: Philippians 2:22

"But you know of his proven character, that he served with me in the furtherance of the Gospel like a child serving his father."

Learn: Timothy was recognized by others for his godly character.

John Morgan said, *"Character is doing the right thing on purpose."* It is the tangible demonstration of our commitment to Christ and the currency of ministry.

We've all seen the casualties caused by those who compromised in their character. We must never seek to advance our cause at the expense of our character.

I heard my friend, Mike Farris, say, *"You can't separate character from the characterization of a person."* Who people experience you to be grows out of who you are.

In other words, who people think you are grows out of who you really are.

In this passage, Paul said two things about Timothy. First, his character was known. Second, his character was proven. The Greek word used means *"validated."* Timothy had proven Himself to others. Proof demands evidence.

Godly character is not asserted; it is demonstrated. The process of character demonstration is generally achieved over time. In this passage, Paul describes Timothy as likeminded, sincere, showing care, selfless, having a proven character, submissive, and a servant.

There is a clear contrast in Philippians 2:21 and 22. Most everyone else thinks mainly about themselves. But Timothy proved himself to be different. That's why Paul said, I have *"no one else"* like him (Philippians 2:20).

Apply:

Does your character demonstrate your faith?

_____

_____

_____

_____

How would others describe your faith?

_____

_____

_____

_____

_____

_____

_____

Day Two

Read: Acts 16:2

"and he was well spoken of by the brothers and sisters who were in Lystra and Iconium."

Learn: Timothy was well-spoken of.

Yesterday, we saw in Philippians 2:20 that Paul said of Timothy, *"I have no one like him."* Have you ever heard anyone say that about someone else? Maybe you've said it this way: *"I've never met anyone like him or her."*

Philippians 2 explains what Paul said of Timothy. Acts 16:2 describes what others said of him.

Others spoke well of Timothy. We see from this passage how Paul, as well as the people of Philippi, Lystra, and Iconium, respected Timothy. The difference is that Timothy lived in Lystra. They knew him.

Scripture reveals that Timothy was well spoken of by the leaders of the church and the people. What do the people who know you best say about you?

Jesus asked a similar question to His disciples in Matthew 16. He asked, *"Who do people say that the Son of Man is?"* The disciples gave several answers. Then, Jesus asked a more personal question and asked them, *"Who do you say that I am?"* The answer from the disciples was noticeably different than that which was given by the people.

Have you ever been asked to complete a personal recommendation for someone? When people make that request, they want information about someone from an individual who has personal knowledge of the person. If the Holy Spirit were writing your reference letter, *what would He say about you?*

Apply:

What do people say about you?

_____

_____

_____

_____

_____

_____

_____

What about the people who know you best?

_____

_____

_____

_____

_____

_____

_____

Day Three

Read: I Timothy 5:23

"Do not go on drinking only water but use a little wine for the sake of your stomach and your frequent ailments."

Learn: Timothy's convictions demonstrated his faith.

This verse talks about Timothy's character through his actions. Our character is revealed by what we do. The verse suggests that Timothy had abstained from drinking alcohol based on a personal conviction. Evidently, Timothy lived an exemplary life in accordance with his convictions.

Paul had given instructions to the churches about alcohol. Those instructions included certain precautions about it (see Romans 14:21; 1 Corinthians 6:9-10, 12; Galatians 5:21; Ephesians 5:18; 1 Timothy 3:3, 8).

Convenience or even comfort isn't an excuse for compromise. Paul said in Romans 14:14 that if I have a conviction about something *(even if it isn't wrong for someone else)* and I do it, for me it is sin. I'm not suggesting that Paul was tempting Timothy to sin. I am suggesting that Timothy was courageous for living his convictions.

Apply:

Read Jeremiah 35:1-14. What convictions did the Rechabites have and how did they follow them? What does Romans 14:14 say about living out our convictions?

_____

_____

_____

_____

_____

_____

_____

How does your faith impact the way that you live or decisions you make?

_____

_____

_____

_____

_____

_____

_____

Day Four

Read: 1 Corinthians 4:17

"For this reason, I have sent to you Timothy, who is my beloved and faithful child in the Lord, and he will remind you of my ways which are in Christ, as I teach everywhere in every church."

Learn: Paul had full confidence in Timothy.

Who is the person you look to when you really need someone?

This verse expresses Paul's confidence in Timothy. In the verse immediately before this one, Paul instructed the church to "imitate me." Then he said to them, "That's why I sent Timothy to you." Paul believed that Timothy would represent his message faithfully to the church. Timothy would teach the same message that Paul taught.

Last week, we looked at how Paul worked with Timothy in 11 locations and sent Timothy to five by himself. The reason Paul had no concern about sending Timothy to these places was because he had full confidence in him and his message. It is as though Paul was saying, *"I know what he is going to say to you."*

That's why Paul had full confidence in him. Timothy was Dependable!

Apply:

Do you believe other people believe they can depend on you?

Day Five

Read: 1 Timothy 3:14-15

"I am writing these things to you, hoping to come to you before long; ¹⁵ but in case I am delayed, I write so that you will know how one should act in the household of God, which is the church of the living God, the pillar and support of the truth."

Learn: Timothy was still growing in his faith.

Timothy, like most of us, wasn't where he needed to be spiritually yet. Remember, even the Apostle Paul said that of himself (Philippians 3:12). However, it is important to remember that though Paul wasn't where he needed to be, he was making progress.

Most of us need to make progress spiritually.

Paul wrote these things to Timothy so that he would know how to live as God instructed. Note that the text doesn't say that *"they"* will know, but that *"you"* will know. Paul's instructions would help Timothy know how people should behave in the church. Since Timothy was going to be in a position of leading people, Paul's instructions would help Timothy in his leadership.

This passage reveals that Timothy was still learning. He needed the more mature leadership of Paul to help him navigate the responsibility that God had entrusted to him. Paul was not fussing at Timothy for not knowing; he was discipling him.

There were two things Paul wanted Timothy to know. First, he wanted Timothy to know that it is God's church. It's His household, His church, and His truth. Second, Paul wanted Timothy to know that ministry is about Him. Verse 15 is a remnant of an early Christological hymn. The *"mystery of godliness"* is about Christ. He was revealed in the flesh, vindicated in the Spirit, appeared to angels, preached among nations, believed in the world, and taken up to glory.

> *When Paul wanted to help Timothy*
> *in his administration in the church,*
> *he quoted a HYMN!*

Music can have such a powerful impact on faith. This is why it is so important that the lyrics of our music compliment and even inform what we believe. It's how some believers grow in their faith.

Apply:

In what areas do you need to grow?

Week Three

Overcome!

Anyone who has flown in an airplane is familiar with the pre-flight routine. Typically, as the plane is taxiing down the runway, before take-off, a flight attendant will review the preflight safety instructions. These include fastening your seatbelt, instructions regarding emergency exits and oxygen masks, where to place your carry-on luggage, the location of flotation devices, and other instructions. Certain airlines include instructions on the *"brace position."* Passengers are told that they might be instructed to assume the *"brace position"* if there is the threat of a crash or emergency landing.

The world can be a dangerous place. We all face obstacles, but we don't always get the chance to brace for impact before they strike. How we handle obstacles demonstrates a lot about our faith.

The third benchmark of the Christian life is standing in your faith.

Paul described a number of obstacles that Timothy faced in his life and ministry. Some of the obstacles he faced pertained to circumstances that were beyond his control. Yet, despite these obstacles, we find a quiet strength in Timothy. Through his example, we learn lessons on how to stand in our faith in the face of obstacles.

Day One

Read: Acts 16:1

"Now Paul also came to Derbe and to Lystra. And a disciple was there, named Timothy, the son of a Jewish woman who was a believer, but his father was a Greek,"

Learn: Timothy lived his faith despite obstacles he encountered.

Timothy seems to have been reared in a home where only one parent shared his faith. This seems to have been significant enough of an obstacle that Paul thought it best to have Timothy circumcised to demonstrate the authenticity of his faith.

Every family has its own unique issues. How do you handle adversities in your family?

God's plan is clear. He desires for homes to be established on faith where both parents share and demon-

54

strate their faith. Paul warned in 2 Corinthians 6:14 about the danger of being unequally yoked. Though this context of this passage is not about marriage, the same truth could apply.

The Old Testament, in several places, gives instructions about marrying outside the community of faith (Deuteronomy 7:3-4; Joshua 23:12; Ezra 9-10). Additionally, the Bible presents Solomon's many marriages with foreign women as part of what led to sin (1 Kings 11; 16-19).

The Bible is clear: families work best when we follow God's plan. Unfortunately, that doesn't seem to have been the case with Timothy. Perhaps that has not worked out like you hoped it would in your life. God protected and used Timothy, and He can do the same for you.

Apply:

What obstacles are you facing that you need God's help to overcome?

_____

_____

_____

_____

_____

_____

_____

Day Two

Read: Hebrews 13:23

"Know that our brother Timothy has been released, with whom, if he comes soon, I will see you."

Learn: Timothy maintained his faith even in difficult circumstances.

In this verse, we learn that Timothy was likely suffering for the Gospel. Despite the difficulties of his circumstances, Timothy continued to serve the Lord.

The text does not record why Timothy was imprisoned, but the implication is that it was because of his faithfulness to the Gospel. He was faithful even if being faithful cost him something.

Mark Batterson said, *"So often, we want everything God offers without having to give anything up."* A person of faithfulness stands in his or her faith even when difficulties arise.

Timothy's death is not recorded in the Bible. According to extrabiblical church tradition, Timothy remained in Ephesus for the rest of his life, until he was martyred for his faith.

In fact, that's exactly what Paul urged his young protégé to do — to stay in Ephesus and battle the false teaching that was occurring there (1 Timothy 1:1).

Apply:

Would you say that you exemplify a proven character?

_____

_____

_____

_____

_____

_____

_____

Do you maintain your faith even in bad circumstances?

_____

_____

_____

_____

_____

_____

_____

Day Three

Read: 1 Timothy 4:12

"Let no one look down on your youthfulness, but rather in speech, conduct, love, faith, and purity, show yourself an example of those who believe."

Learn: Timothy had some obstacles in his life that were outside of his control.

All of us face issues that are outside of our control. In this passage, Paul was admonishing Timothy to model his faith. The implication is that Paul was instructing Timothy not to give anyone cause to criticize him because of his age.

Timothy was young. There wasn't very much he could do about that. He was probably in his late 20's or early 30's when this letter was written. He lived in a culture that respected age. It's not clear if Paul is referencing issues people actually had with Timothy or if Paul was simply admonishing Timothy not to give anyone reasons to have concerns with him.

Perhaps, like Jeremiah, Timothy recognized he had not earned respect from some people in the congregation. *So, how did Paul advise Timothy to combat his youthfulness?* He encouraged him to be an example.

Paul exhorted him to not give them cause to despise Timothy because he was young.

Timothy couldn't control his age or what others thought about him, but he could control how he lived. Paul encouraged him to conduct himself as he knew he should.

Apply:

How do you handle issues that you can't control?

_____

_____

_____

_____

_____

_____

Day Four

Read: 1 Timothy 5:23

"Do not go on drinking only water but use a little wine for the sake of your stomach and your frequent ailments."

Learn: Timothy had some physical health concerns.

We saw last week that Timothy abstained from alcohol for spiritual reasons. That is admirable. However, in this passage, we are told that Timothy had stomach issues.

We are not told what kind of stomach concerns Timothy had. However, the text states that they were *"frequent."* The implication of Paul's statement in this passage is that Timothy believed so strongly in his convictions that he held to them even if those convictions were costly.

Paul isn't asking Timothy to compromise a conviction for physical benefit, he is concerned for his health. Not every day serving the Lord is sunny and pain-free. Some days are cloudy and painful. But we must not let physical discomfort prevent us from spiritual obedience.

When Satan received divine permission to torment Job, it was the attack on his health that seemed to weaken Job even more than the attack on his family and wealth. It can be hard to serve when you don't feel well.

To be sure, some physical maladies are real and must be addressed. However, is it possible that some physical circumstances we cite as reasons for not serving the Lord are excuses more than they are reasons?

Apply:

How can physical discomfort prevent us from serving the Lord?

_____

_____

_____

A LIFE DEAR TO GOD

_____

_____

_____

_____

Day Five

Read: 2 Timothy 1:7

"For God has not given us a spirit of timidity, but of power and love and discipline."

Learn: Timothy may have struggled with fear.

Fear can be a griping obstacle. It may be the most common struggle believers face. We all face fears in our lives. We face fears related to health, finances, relationships, occupations, the unknown, the future, and many more.

In this passage, Paul is either addressing a real or potential fear that Timothy had. He made a similar statement in 1 Corinthians 16:10 about Timothy and fear. It seems that either Timothy had some issues with fear or Paul was concerned that he might.

I have often heard and seen on the internet the claim that the Bible says, "Do Not Fear" 365 times. That's one for each day, they claim. The only problem is, if you look up that phrase in your Bible program, depending on your translation, you will discover that the Bible actually only uses that phrase between 75 and 100 times.

Besides, even if it were true that the Bible made that claim 365 times, once every 4 years on February 29th, we'd feel like it wasn't covered (since the leap year has 366 days)!

It is true that the Bible often states, ***"Do not fear."***

The word Paul used in 2 Timothy 1:7 really means *"cowardice."* It's not clear if Timothy was running away from anything or if Paul was afraid that he might.

Read Acts 13:13 and 15:36-41. *What was Paul's response to Mark leaving during his first missionary journey?* Mark left after things started to get uncomfortable on the missionary journey. Many New Testament scholars have speculated that the reason Mark left was out of fear.

Fear is natural. It is not necessarily a lack of faith. But sometimes living our faith means trusting God even when we are afraid. Paul was saying to Timothy, that spirit of fear, the one that makes you want to quit or walk away, that's not from God. Instead, God wants to give you power, love, and a sound mind.

What do you do when the pain comes? When the trials come? What about when the problems, bills, or medical issues arise? What would it take to turn you away?

Apply:

How can physical discomfort prevent us from serving the Lord?

_____

_____

_____

_____

_____

_____

_____

Week Four

Serve!

In 1 Corinthians 12:12, Paul talked about the parts of the body. In the context, he was explaining how God has gifted each of us differently. We don't have the same gifts, but the differing gifts do not reflect differing importance. There are many different functions in the ministry of the church.

Churches are blessed by many faithful men and women who serve in areas most people will never see.

In Exodus 33, Moses was meeting with the Lord in the context of a great sin on the part of the people of Israel.

Moses was pleading with the Lord in the Tabernacle not to depart from them. The passage describes both an immediate function as Moses interceded for the people but also reflects a pattern of Moses speaking with the Lord. As Moses entered the Tabernacle, the Bible says that the people worshiped at the doors of their tents because they all knew the significance of those divine encounters. After he spoke with the Lord, Moses went out to speak to the people.

But not everyone was there to hear Moses' report of his encounters with the Lord. Joshua, his assistant, stayed in the Tabernacle.

While Moses was out speaking, Joshua remained in the Tabernacle serving. Perhaps he was carrying out necessary functions in the Tabernacle. Perhaps he was learning lessons that would serve him years later when God chose him as Moses' replacement.

Whatever he was doing, it is clear he was following instructions he had been given. Long before Joshua was a leader, he was a servant.

The fourth benchmark of the Christian life is service.

We are all called to be servants of the Lord and to use our giftedness and talents to accomplish His purpose.

We learn from Timothy lessons we all need to apply to our lives about our own roles in service to the Lord.

Day One

Read: Acts 16:3

"Paul wanted this man to leave with him, and he took him and circumcised him because of the Jews who were in those parts, for they all knew that his father was a Greek."

Learn: Timothy was who Paul was looking for to serve on his team.

This passage begins with the phrase, "Paul wanted Timothy to go with him." That's a compelling statement. It's not clear if Paul knew Timothy prior to Acts 16:1. However, something about Timothy so impressed Paul that he wanted Timothy on his team.

If you were drafting a baseball team, what would you look for? You'd probably look for people who could play different positions, some with fielding ability and others with speed. You'd probably want some on your team who are left- handed and others who are right-handed. You'd want some who could bat with a high batting average and others who could hit with power. You also want starting pitching, a closer, pinch hitting, and more.

Now suppose you were drafting a team for ministry. What would you be looking for? What types of gifts and talents would you want people to possess on your team?

Paul wanted Timothy on his team. That's why he wanted Timothy to be circumcised (probably because his father was a Greek and this would avoid questions anyone might have about his convictions). What's not stated in the text is Timothy's willingness to do it.

Paul saw something in Timothy and wanted him on his team. Timothy's willingness to be circumcised to join the team demonstrates what Paul already had seen in him.

Apply:

What gifts do you bring to God's team?

_____

_____

_____

_____

_____

Are there sacrifices you are willing to make in order to be used of God?

_____

_____

_____

_____

_____

_____

_____

Day Two

Read: Romans 16:21; 1 Thessalonians 3:2

"Timothy, my fellow worker, greets you."

"And we sent Timothy, our brother and God's fellow worker in the Gospel of Christ, to strengthen and encourage you for the benefit of your faith."

Learn: Timothy was a co-laborer with Paul.

It's clear that Paul was the leader of the team. Timothy was serving with Paul, but he knew it was Paul's team. Yet Paul considered Timothy his *"co-worker."*

We know from Scripture that they served together in Phrygia, Galatia, Mysia, Troas, Thessalonica, Philippi, Berea, Athens, Corinth, Macedonia, Ephesus, and Asia. Several of those were difficult assignments.

Timothy served faithfully with Paul. That's part of the reason why Paul trusted him so much.

Sometimes, Timothy's responsibility was to strengthen and encourage the believers in their faith. At other times it was merely to bring greetings on behalf of Paul. How faithfully do you serve when you don't set the agenda?

Apply:

Are you willing to serve when it's not always noticed?

_____

_____

_____

_____

_____

_____

_____

Day Three

Read: Acts 18:5

"But when Silas and Timothy came down from Macedonia, Paul began devoting himself completely to the word, testifying to the Jews that Jesus was the Christ."

Learn: Timothy freed up Paul to do work Paul needed to do.

The church staff with whom I have the privilege of working serve in many areas throughout the week. They work in music, Sunday school, Wednesday night activities, preschool, children, youth, young adults, special needs, senior adults, technology, pastoral care, hospital visitation, some writing letters or calling people, benevolence, special ministries, taking care of our facilities, and more.

Think about a normal Sunday morning. People open and close the building, make and serve coffee, serve in the parking lot, on the safety team, as greeters, at the welcome desks, as ushers, make and serve food in classes, and often between or after services.

We have many who teach Sunday School or assist in those classes. Our worship service is blessed by those who lead, play, or sing the music, work in sound or on camera, coordinate the PowerPoint, lighting, live-stream, Facebook, or announcements. Others collect and count money, count people, prepare for baptisms, serve in the nursery, and more.

Throughout the week, others plan and prepare for services, clean building, serve needs of people, coordinate benevolence and other ministries. In add-ition, there are also special ministries like weddings, funerals, graduations, concerts, meetings, etc.

We have music programs, youth programs, young adult programs, children's programs, committees, and so much more. Then there are special events like Vacation Bible School that require all hands-on deck and an army of volunteers.

On top of all that, the work of ministry requires staff to pray, study, plan, organize, meet with people, contact people, share the Gospel with people, and what is often one of the most critical things to do in ministry ⎯➤**THINK.**

In addition, some churches (like the one where I am privileged to serve) have other organizations like special needs or preschool programs that meet regularly throughout the week. Finally, some faithful servants of the Lord serve in areas most will never see.

That's just a normal week. And, let's face it, most weeks aren't normal!

But we all know that the ministry of the church is not about us or our areas of ministry; it is about Christ. It's His church, and we all use our time, talents, gifts, and resources for His glory!

Read: Exodus 33:11

There would come a day when Joshua would be the leader, but throughout the first part of his ministry, he served Moses. Similarly, there would come a day when Timothy would be the pastor of the church at Ephesus, but for much of his ministry, he served in areas that assisted Paul. Ministry is not about who is most important; it's about the calling and gifting of God.

God might be preparing you today for something He will use you to do tomorrow. Or, He might have perfectly suited you to serve right where you are. He might use you to lead, or He might use you to serve those who do. Where has God called you to serve?

Apply:

Do you serve in a way that helps others serve more effectively?

_____

_____

_____

_____

_____

_____

_____

Day Four

Read: Acts 20:1-6

"After the uproar had ceased, Paul sent for the disciples, and when he had encouraged them and taken his leave of them, he left to go to Macedonia. ² *When he had gone through those regions and had given them much encouragement, he came to Greece. And there he spent three months, and when a plot was formed against him by the Jews as he was about to set sail for Syria, he decided to return through Macedonia.* ⁴ *And he was accompanied by Sopater of Berea, the son of Pyrrhus, and by Aristarchus and Secundus of the Thessalonians, and Gaius of Derbe, and Timothy, and Tychicus and Trophimus of Asia. Now these had gone on ahead and were waiting for us at Troas.* ⁶ *We sailed from Philippi after the days of Unleavened Bread and reached them at Troas within five days, and we stayed there for seven days."*

Learn: Sometimes Timothy came alongside Paul, and sometimes he went ahead to prepare the way.

This is a somewhat complicated passage. It is unclear exactly who is going ahead of Paul and who is staying with him. Some have suggested that most of this group was sent ahead and that Luke and perhaps others stayed with Paul as something of a protection detail.

Some went and some stayed. Those who went prepared the way and waited for Paul's arrival. Timothy seems to have been among them. Their job was to prepare the way for Paul and to wait until he arrived.

Meanwhile, Paul was celebrating the Festival of Passover and Unleavened Bread. Note that those who went ahead seem to have missed out on the celebration of the Passover.

Sometimes, helping others requires that I miss out on some things.

Apply:

Are you willing to serve unnoticed?

_____

_____

_____

_____

_____

_____

_____

Day Five

Read: 2 Corinthians 1:19

"For the Son of God, Christ Jesus, who was preached among you by us — by me and Silvanus and Timothy — was not yes and no but has been yes in Him."

Learn: Timothy preached a consistent message to that of Paul.

Paul's lesson in this passage to the church in Corinth is about the consistency of our witness even amidst the uncertainties of life. Paul's plans had changed, but his message was consistent.

Moreover, Paul affirmed that whether the message was preached by him, Silvanus, or Timothy, it was the same. Paul could trust what Timothy would say.

We live in a world that loves to hear itself talk. We also love to look at ourselves too *(i.e., "selfies"),* but that's a story for another time. Social media provides the platform and feeds our desire to be heard. Today, artificial intelligence will even craft the message for you.

It's worth noting that Paul tells us that Timothy co-wrote 2 Corinthians, Philemon, 1 and 2 Thessalonians, and was with Paul in the writing of Romans. Yet, those are all called letters of Paul, and rightly so.

We, frankly, don't know how much input Timothy had on those letters. But we know Paul had confidence that when Timothy spoke, he spoke the same message as Paul.

Apply:

Can people trust what you say?

_____

_____

_____

_____

_____

_____

_____

*What about when you talk about your faith? Do you have
enough information to speak convincingly about your
faith and can people trust that you will share your faith
with others?*

_____

_____

_____

_____

_____

_____

_____

Go!

Bible students know that there is only one imperative in the Great Commission (Matthew 28:18-20). It is the command to make disciples. The other verbs, including the verb to go, are participles. However, most Greek scholars understand these participles to carry the imperatival force of the verb to make disciples. So, involved in the process of making disciples is the anticipation of going.

In one sense, the instruction conveys the idea of *"as you go ... make disciples."* This suggests that all along our walk of faith, we should be making disciples. In another sense, this word involves intentionality. We are called to "go" with a purpose of making disciples. I believe both are understood in Jesus' instructions to His disciples.

This week, we are looking at being on mission for Christ. We'll see how Timothy was trusted by Paul and sent on several missionary appointments in Paul's place.

The identifying feature of Timothy's life that Paul notes qualifies him for this mission was his genuine care for the spiritual condition of people. That drove Timothy's availability to be used.

At our core, Christians are called to be missional people. It may be that God wants to use you on mission "as you go" this week. Or, it may be that God has a specific task on which He intends to send you. *Are you willing to go on mission for Christ?*

Day One

Read: Acts 19:21-22

"Now after these things were finished, Paul resolved in the Spirit to go to Jerusalem after he had passed through Macedonia and Achaia, saying, "After I have been there, I must also see Rome." [22] And after he sent into Macedonia two of those who assisted him, Timothy and Erastus, he himself stayed in Asia for a while."

Learn: Go as you are sent.

In this passage, Paul was making plans that would lead to what many people believe was the final journey of his life. He was given direction by the Holy Spirit that altered his plans and the course of his life. This plan included an ultimate goal (Rome) but had several steps between where he was and there.

The first step was Macedonia. Paul had been to Macedonia before (cf. Acts 16:9-11). Macedonia included: Berea, Thessalonica, Philippi, Amphipolis, Apollonia, Neapolis, and Nicopolis.

Macedonia had been a place of great opportunity and discovery (the conversion of Lydia, the conversion of the jailer and his family, and the noble believers in Berea). But it was also a place of persecution and opposition. He was beaten and imprisoned in Philippi, opposed and threatened in Thessalonica, and eventually forcibly driven out of the city in Berea. Now Paul wanted to go back. And God apparently used that visit in a profound way. The believers in Macedonia apparently collected an offering that supported Paul's final journey to Rome (Romans 15:24–28).

But before Paul could get to Macedonia, he sent Timothy ahead of him to prepare the way. We don't know what all Timothy did to prepare, but Paul trusted him so completely that whatever needed to be accomplished or prepared, Timothy would get it done.

Timothy would complete whatever and everything that needed to be done for Paul's ministry to be a success.

Apply:

God doesn't always give you a job description delineating every detail of His plan for your life. But are you faithful to complete everything He asks of you, even if no one ever knows you did it?

_____

_____

_____

_____

_____

_____

_____

Day Two

Read: 1 Thessalonians 3:1-10

"Therefore, when we could no longer endure it, we thought it best to be left behind, alone at Athens, ² and we sent Timothy, our brother and God's fellow worker in the Gospel of Christ, to strengthen and encourage you for the benefit of your faith, ³ so that no one would be disturbed by these afflictions. For you yourselves know that we have been destined for this. ⁴ For even when we were with you, we kept telling you in advance that we were going to suffer affliction, and so it happened, as you know. ⁵ For this reason, when I could no longer endure it, I also sent to find out about your faith, for fear that the tempter might have tempted you and our labor would be for nothing .⁶ But now that Timothy has come to us from you and has brought us good news of your faith and love, and that you always think kindly of us, longing to see us just as we also long to see you, ⁷ for this reason, brothers and sisters, in all our distress and affliction we were comforted about you through your faith; ⁸ for now we really live, if you stand firm in the Lord. ⁹ For what thanks can we give to God for you in return for all the joy with which we rejoice because

> *of you before our God, [10] as we keep praying most earnestly night and day that we may see your faces and may complete what is lacking in your faith?"*

Learn: Go where others can't.

There are a number of instances in Scripture when Timothy ministered for Paul.

- Timothy was left in Berea after Paul was forced to leave because of persecution.
- During a time of persecution, he is sent to Thessalonica to strengthen the believers in their faith (1 Thessalonians 3:1-3).
- He is sent to Macedonia from Ephesus with a similar mission (Acts 19:22).
- He is sent as Paul's emissary to bring teaching and healing to the troubled church in Corinth (1 Corinthians 4:17-21).
- He was apparently sent to Philippi and perhaps returns with a monetary gift from that church for Paul (Philippians 2:19; 4:15-16; Acts 18:5).
- He was sent by Paul to Ephesus as Pastor and then encouraged to stay to teach them.

In this passage, Paul felt like he needed to stay in Athens. Acts 17:1–13 recounts the conflict that drove Paul from Thessalonica to Berea. Then, according to

Acts 17:14-15, Timothy and Silas stayed in Berea as Paul went on to Athens alone. At some point, before Timothy joined Paul in Athens, apparently, Paul sent him (1 Thessalonians 3:1) back to Thessalonica to see how the believers were doing and bring a report to Paul.

News traveled slowly in the 1st century. Unlike today's instant information, it might take weeks or longer to receive information. But Paul needed to know about their faith (1 Thessalonians 3:5), so he dispatched Timothy, who eventually brought back good news about the believers in Thessalonica. So, Paul concluded that section by reminding the Thessalonians that he was grateful to God for their faith and regularly praying for them.

Timothy's function in this instance was huge for Paul. For whatever reason, he could not return at that time to Thessalonica. It could have been for security reasons or just that the ministry needs in Athens were too pressing. But whatever the reason, Paul found Timothy so dependable, he could trust that Timothy would give the believers in Thessalonica encouragement from Paul and bring back word from them that would encourage the Apostle as well.

Apply:

Do people trust you to serve in their place when they can't?

_____

_____

_____

_____

_____

_____

_____

Day Three

Read: 1 Corinthians 4:15-17; 16:10

"For if you were to have countless tutors in Christ, yet you would not have many fathers, for in Christ Jesus I became your father through the Gospel. [16] *Therefore, I urge you to be imitators of me.* [17] *For this reason I have sent to you Timothy, who is my beloved and faithful child in the Lord, and he will remind you of my ways, which are in Christ, just as I teach everywhere in every church."*

"Now if Timothy comes, see that he has no reason to be afraid while among you, for he is doing the Lord's work, as I also am."

Learn: Go as a representative.

In Star Wars, Episode V: *The Empire Strikes Back*, Darth Vader said to Luke Skywalker, *"I am your father."* Paul made the same claim to the believers in Corinthians (1 Corinthians 4:15). He became their father through the Gospel. That is, he brought spiritual life to them through the Gospel.

Then, like a good father, Paul wanted them to learn from him by imitating his faith. Like young children, they would learn how to grow in the Lord by imitating him.

But Paul was unable to go to Corinth physically. Instead, he sent Timothy. Paul said, *"That's why I sent Timothy to you."* That's also why Paul wanted the believers in Corinth to take care of Timothy (1 Corinthians 16:10), because Timothy was that valuable.

Paul wanted the believers in Corinth to imitate him, so he sent Timothy. That suggests a great deal of confidence in Timothy to know that he would assist them in imitating Paul. So, when Timothy modeled faith in Corinth and the believers responded, they were not imitating Timothy; they were imitating the one Timothy was imitating.

In 1 Corinthians 11:1, Paul shared a similar message with Corinth when he instructed them to imitate him as he imitated Christ. But he was not there physically to model that faith. That's where Timothy came in. He imitated Paul in the same way that Paul imitated Christ.

Paul said, in 2 Corinthians 5:20, we are ambassadors for Christ. As you go, make sure you represent Christ well.

Apply:

Can people trust that if they mimic your faith, they are actually imitating Christ?

_____

_____

_____

_____

_____

_____

_____

Do you draw attention to yourself or to Christ?

_____

_____

_____

_____

_____

_____

_____

Day Four

Read: Philippians 2:19-24

"But I hope, in the Lord Jesus, to send Timothy to you shortly, so that I also may be encouraged when I learn of your condition. [20] For I have no one else of kindred spirit who will genuinely be concerned for your welfare. [21] For they all seek after their own interests, not those of Christ Jesus. [22] But you know of his proven character, that he served with me in the furtherance of the Gospel like a child serving his father. [23] Therefore I hope to send him immediately, as soon as I see how things go with me; [24] and I trust in the Lord that I myself will also be coming shortly."

Learn: Go because you care.

Just like Paul wanted to know how the believers were doing in Thessalonica, Paul had the same concern for those in Philippi. So, he determined to send Timothy to find out how they were doing.

Paul believed that learning about their faith would be a source of encouragement for him. But he also knew something else — Timothy genuinely cared for them.

Going on mission demands caring for people.

Paul highlights the contrast between Timothy and so many others. Most people care about themselves. Timothy cared for others. It was one of the fundamental reasons why He was so helpful for Paul.

Timothy was reliable. In his writings, Paul described him as a brother, a son, a co-worker, a fellow soldier, and a messenger. Here he is someone who cares.

Apply:

Do you genuinely care about people enough to serve them?

_____

_____

_____

_____

_____

_____

_____

Day Five

Read: Acts 17:14-15

"Then immediately the brothers sent Paul out to go as far as the sea, and Silas and Timothy remained there. ¹⁵ Now those who escorted Paul brought him as far as Athens, and receiving a command for Silas and Timothy to come to him as soon as possible, they left."

Learn: Go where you are needed.

Sometimes serving the Lord simply involves our availability. Timothy was there for his mentor when Paul needed him. Jesus said that when the Son of Man comes in His glory, He will pronounce blessing on the faithful sheep. He said, *"Then the King will say to those on His right side ... I was in prison and you came to Me"* (Matthew 25:34–36). It is a mark of a faithful servant. That's who Timothy was for Paul.

Timothy was the guy Paul turned to when he needed something done or he needed someone with him quickly. He came to Paul in prison at least three times. When Paul was in Philippi, Timothy visited him (Acts 16; Philippians 2:19; 1 Timothy 3:6). Next, when Paul was imprisoned in Caesarea, where many scholars believe Paul wrote the letters to Philemon and Colossians, Timothy was there with him.

Then, Paul was imprisoned in Rome where he sent for Timothy (2 Timothy 4:21) and Timothy undoubtedly would have accommodated Paul's request.

When Paul was forced to leave Berea because of the persecution, he left Timothy there. Paul went to Athens alone. Then, Paul sent instructions for Timothy to join him in Athens.

Paul's instructions came with an urgency. He asked them to instruct Timothy to come quickly. This would not be the last time Paul called for his disciple to come quickly (cf. 2 Timothy 4:21).

Think about a time in your life when you needed someone to come quickly. Who did you turn to? *Who would you turn to now if the need arose again?*

Apply:

Who would you turn to when you really needed someone? What is it about them that makes them trustworthy?

_____

_____

_____

_____

_____

_____

_____

Are you the kind of person people can turn to when they need something in a hurry?

_____

_____

_____

_____

_____

_____

_____

Encourage!

Everyone needs encouragement—*Everyone.* Think about that in your own life. Do you remember times in your life when you really needed an encouraging word? Maybe you are walking through that right now.

Paul often asked people to pray for him (Romans 15:20-32; 2 Corinthians 1:10-11; Ephesians 6:18-20; Philippians 1:19; Colossians 4:2-4; 1 Thessalonians 5:25; 2 Thessalonians 3:1-2; Philemon 1:22).

But it's not just difficult times in our lives when we need encouragement. We regularly need it. Timothy was an encourager for Paul in many ways, and Paul recognized it. When you have experienced those times of encouragement in your life, you know it. They are God-sent blessings.

This week, our challenge is to learn to be an encourager. In the same way that Timothy ministered to Paul, you can minister to others. I hope that as you walk through the lessons this week, the Lord will lay on your mind people in whose lives you can invest.

The writer of Hebrews (Hebrews 3:13) admonished us to "encourage one another every day, as long as it is still called "today." I suspect that means, as long as you are alive, or until Jesus returns, be an encourager.

The Bible is full of men and women who were encouragers: Jethro, Jonathan, Barzillai, Elizabeth, Mary, Joanna, and Susanna (Luke 8:2-3), Barnabas, Paul, Judas, and Silas (Acts 15:32), Philemon, Lydia, Onesiphorus, Timothy, and many others.

The ultimate work on encouragement in our lives comes through the ministry of the Holy Spirit. But there are also times when God uses you and me.

Paul said, *"Now that Timothy has come to us from you"* (1 Thessalonians 3:6). We're going to see this week the times when Timothy came to Paul when Paul needed him. His example remains a challenge for us. God is calling you to encourage someone this week.

Day One

Read: 1 Timothy 1:2

"To Timothy, my true son in the faith: grace, mercy, and peace from God the Father and Christ Jesus our Lord."

Learn: Timothy encouraged Paul by their unique relationship.

One of the phrases Paul used to describe Timothy was, *"my true son."* That says something of Timothy's character and their relationship. As far as we know, Paul never married or had any children, but seems to be saying of Timothy, *"If I had a son, I'd want him to be like you."*

Timothy was a true friend. The word *"true"* means genuine or real. That phrase suggests context that Paul does not give us. It suggests time together, dependability, authenticity, as well as many experiences that they shared together.

Often you know the quality of your friendship with someone when difficulties arise. Proverbs 17:17 says, *"A friend loves at all times."* Perhaps Paul was thinking about some people that he thought were his friends but who proved otherwise when things got difficult. Near the end of his life, Paul was keenly aware of those who were not with him (Timothy 1:15; 4:9–12).

In God's kindness, He gives us friends. If you have at least one true friend, you are blessed.

Apply:

Who in your life is a true friend? Spend time today thanking God for your friends.

_____

_____

_____

_____

_____

_____

_____

Day Two

Read: 2 Timothy 1:4

"longing to see you, even as I recall your tears, so that I may be filled with joy."

Learn: Timothy encouraged Paul by his tender affection.

Paul told Timothy that he was *"mindful of [his] tears."*

The text does not specify the reason for Timothy's tears. Perhaps Timothy was aware of Paul's imprisonment, grieved by Paul's departure (1 Timothy 1:3), moved by Paul's emotional farewell in Ephesus (Acts 20:37), or anticipating Paul's imminent death (2 Timothy 4:6-8).

In the middle of a difficult time, David expressed confidence that God was aware of his sorrow. He proclaimed by faith that *"you have put my tears in your bottle"* (Psalms 56:8). That was David's way of expressing that God remembers our tears. It was his confidence that God knows our pain, He feels our pain, and He is moved by our pain.

Believers take confidence today that God knows our pain. He knows when we cry (Psalms 30:5), and He promises to hear when we cry (Psalms 34:15; Joel 2:12). Christians take confidence in the fact that we never cry alone.

There are numerous accounts in Scripture that reveal God's providential care in our pain. God heard when Hagar (Genesis 21:7), Abraham (Genesis 23:2), Hannah (1 Samuel 1:10), David and Jonathan (1 Samuel 20:41), Hezekiah (2 Kings 20:7), a grieving widow (Luke 7:13), a repentant woman (Luke 7:38), Mary, the grieving sister of Lazarus (John 11:28-34), Peter (Matthew 26:75), Mary, the mother of Jesus (John 20:11-15), and Jesus (John 11:35, Luke 19:41, Hebrews 5:7; cf. Isaiah 53:7) cried. He hears your tears.

Paul was aware of Timothy's tears. It expresses the personal aspect of their relationship. The frequent use of the second- person pronoun ("you") in verses 3-5 emphasizes the closeness of their friendship. Remembering those tears brought about a desire, again, in Paul to see his young friend. Timothy's tears

110

reminded Paul of the blessing of a close friend.

Solomon explained that there is a time for tears (Ecclesiastes 3:4). But praise the Lord, John recorded a voice from the throne of God reminding us that there will come a day when God will *"wipe away every tear from their eyes"* (Revelation 21:3-5).

Have you ever been encouraged by tears?

Apply:

Is there someone God is leading you to encourage this week?

Day Three

Read: Acts 18:5

"But when Silas and Timothy came down from Macedonia, Paul began devoting himself completely to the word, testifying to the Jews that Jesus was the Christ."

Learn: Timothy encouraged Paul by freeing him up to focus his time on what God called him to do.

When Paul went to Corinth in Acts 18, he served for a while bi-vocationally. Paul worked as a tent maker with Aquila and Priscilla.

There is a transition in the text in 18:5. It happened when Silas and Timothy arrived. They had been left behind in Berea (Acts 17:14–15). It's likely that when they arrived, Silas and Timothy brought with them an offering from the churches to support Paul's ministry (cf. 2 Corinthians 11:18; Philippians 4:15).

Whether it was money or just their presence, the arrival of Silas and Timothy emboldened Paul to concentrate all of his time and focus on preaching the Gospel. Their timely arrival encouraged Paul in his ministry. They freed him up to focus all of his time and energy on the Gospel.

All of us have spiritual leaders in our lives whom God has used to disciple us and strengthen us. It might be that God could use you to be an encouragement in their lives. We all need encouragement. That encouragement could come from you in many ways. Pray that God would use you to encourage those spiritual leaders in your life.

Apply:

What are some ways God could use you to be an encourager for spiritual leaders?

_____

_____

_____

_____

_____

Day Four

Read: 1 Thessalonians 3:6

"But now that Timothy has come to us from you and has brought us good news of your faith and love, and that you always think kindly of us, longing to see us just as we also long to see you."

Learn: Timothy encouraged Paul by reminding him of how God had used him in the lives of others.

The phrase, *"Now that he has come,"* stands out in this passage for me. The idea is that something was different after Timothy arrived. There was a tangible impact on Paul because Timothy arrived.

We've all seen the opposite. Imagine the scene: you are in a room filled with people, and someone walks in who negatively impacts the entire room. Maybe it is the countenance or their attitude, but something about them affects everyone there.

115

But when Timothy arrived ... he impacted the situation for good. This is likely the same event as is described in Acts 18:5. Very likely, Timothy brought a financial gift for Paul that supported his work. But that is not all. Timothy also brought news about their faith, confirmation that they positively remembered Paul, and the comforting assurance that they desired to see Paul.

Now look at the results of that in Paul's life. Paul said,

- Even in our affliction, we are comforted (Paul was in prison when he wrote that),
- Your testimony gives purpose to our ministry ("we really live if you stand firm in the Lord"),
- We are thankful to God for the joy we receive "from you, and"
- We are praying for you.

Remember Paul's visit to Thessalonica? It wasn't really that great. Some believed (Acts 17:4), but the people there were not as noble-minded as those in Berea (Acts 17:11); a mob broke out threatening violence against Paul and Silas (Acts 17:5); they persecuted a believer named Jason (Acts 17:6); and Paul was smuggled away from the city at night (Acts 17:10).

Despite all that, the people had fond memories of Paul, and he had fond memories of them. Timothy reminded

Paul of that. That could have been a negative ministry experience for Paul. How often has the enemy used experiences like that to make people feel like their ministries are a failure? But God reminded Paul that his ministry there made a difference. And yours does, too! God is using you in ways you may not even know. Maybe we just need more Timothy's to remind us of that.

Apply:

Do you remind others of God's blessings?

_____

_____

_____

_____

_____

_____

_____

Day Five

Read: 2 Timothy 4:9-13

"Make every effort to come to me soon; [10] *for Demas, having loved this present world, has deserted me and gone to Thessalonica; Crescens has gone to Galatia, Titus to Dalmatia.* [11] *Only Luke is with me. Take along Mark and bring him with you, for he is useful to me for service.* [12] *But I have sent Tychicus to Ephesus.* [13] *When you come, bring the overcoat which I left at Troas with Carpus, and the books, especially the parchments."*

Learn: Timothy encouraged Paul by being there at the end.

This was not the first time Paul sent a request for Timothy to come quickly. We saw that earlier in Acts 17:14–15. In this case, given his incarceration, the need was urgent again. But it is even more pressing in that the end of Paul's life was near.

Paul was not asking for Timothy's sympathy. He was asking for his help. This was not just a dying wish from an elderly statesman. It was a request for Timothy to provide him what he needed so Paul could finish well. He was not looking to retire and enjoy what little time he had left. Paul wanted to use every bit of his time for the glory of the Lord.

Paul wanted his coat because he was cold; he wanted his books to study God's Word, and he wanted Timothy to warn him and send him out again in ministry.

At his most vulnerable state in his earthly life, Paul wanted workers, provisions, books, and Timothy. Maybe God can use you to provide something that someone needs. Or maybe God just wants you to be who someone needs.

Often, the ministry of presence is one of the most effective gifts we can give someone.

Apply:

How can you be a person others can count on in their worst times?

A LIFE DEAR TO GOD

_____

_____

_____

_____

_____

_____

A LIFE DEAR TO GOD

Week Seven

Grow!

In 2014, on a sabbatical assignment, my wife and I had the wonderful opportunity of serving in the Philippines. We lived on the campus of a Bible College and Seminary in Baguio. I had the privilege of teaching on their campus and preaching in 15 different churches. We also got to see much of their beautiful country.

One of the classes I was invited to teach was on the Pastoral Epistles. I chose to focus the study of those three books on 50 pastoral ministry issues addressed in the books and the 90 imperatives that Paul used to challenge Timothy and Titus in their pastoral assignments.

These letters are full of pastoral admonitions. I envision Paul writing to his two young ministry protégés, thinking about them in his mind as he personalized those instructions for them. I believe even the selection of the location to which he sent them was customized to their personalities, gifts, and the needs of those locations.

Although the letters contain 90 imperatives, there are a few times when Paul paused and gave special direction to his young disciple, Timothy. I want to highlight five of Paul's instructions that seem to be highlighted in the text and then evaluate how they relate to each of us as well.

The focus for this week Is maturing In Christ. Let's listen in as Paul gave instructions to Timothy about maturing in Christ and apply them to our lives.

Day One

Read: 1 Timothy 6:12

"Fight the good fight of faith; take hold of the eternal life to which you were called, and for which you made the good confession in the presence of many witnesses."

Learn: Paul encouraged Timothy to mature in his faith by fighting the good fight of faith.

Fighting the good fight of faith certainly doesn't mean we are to be combative. But if you are a believer in Jesus Christ, there is a fight you are fighting—even if you didn't know you were fighting it.

In 1 Timothy 3 and Titus 1, Paul listed 23 attributes that should characterize every Christian minister. Of those 23 attributes, five relate to the ability to control one's temper! Very obviously, he is telling us something about our attitudes.

Paul is talking about spiritual discipline. This is the same message that Jesus gave to His disciples in Luke 9:23 when He said, *"If anyone desires to come after Me, let him deny himself, take up his cross daily, and follow Me."*

To be sure, there are some things we are to flee. We are told in 2 Timothy 2:22 to flee lust. But we are told to fight the fight of faith. That is not a fight we can run away from. We live in a world that is increasingly hostile to our faith.

The world will likely not celebrate when you live your religious convictions, and they might even oppose them. Sometimes, standing for your faith will seem like a battle. Jude encouraged the believers in Jude 3 to *"earnestly contend for the faith."* The word that Jude used meant to *"agonize"* for the faith.

We can't sit this one out. There is regular, daily exercise that must characterize our Christian lives. It's worth the struggle.

Some of the last words Paul ever wrote reflect on this challenge. Looking back over his life, Paul concluded in 2 Timothy 4:7, *"I have fought the good fight. I have finished the course. I have kept the faith."* May that be the final assessment of all of us.

Apply:

Are you fighting the fight of faith?

_____

_____

_____

_____

_____

_____

_____

Day Two

Read: 1 Timothy 6:20

"Timothy, protect what has been entrusted to you, avoiding worldly, empty chatter and the opposing arguments of what is falsely called 'knowledge.'"

Learn: Paul admonished Timothy to mature in his faith by guarding what was committed to him.

This passage is part of Paul's summation of his first letter to Timothy. So, in one sense, he is wrapping up everything he has taught throughout the letter.

The phrase, "guard what was entrusted to you" is a sort of mixing of metaphors. It involves a military term ("guard") and also a banking term ("entrusted"). The idea of guarding means to remain vigilant; to stay awake and pay attention.

The concept of something being entrusted refers to a deposit. In fact, that is the literal translation of this verse, "guard the deposit." When I put my money in the bank, I trust that they will take good care of it. Paul is referring to something of value that has been entrusted to Timothy, and his responsibility is to take good care of it.

What was entrusted to Timothy? In this context, Paul seems to be referring to the ministry in which God has allowed him to serve.

In that latter part of this same verse, Paul reminded Timothy that one way we stand guard over what has been entrusted to us is by not getting sidetracked on unprofitable matters. Guarding involves turning away from things like idle babbling and contradictions (this is where we get our English word, *"antithesis"* — what is *"against the thesis"*).

Paul used these same two words (guard and entrust) together in two other occasions (2 Timothy 1:12 and 14). In the former, Paul expressed trust that God would guard what he trusted to Him. In the latter, Paul admonished Timothy to do the same with what was entrusted to him.

Our faith, our family, our spiritual gifts, our ministry opportunities, our time, even our physical possessions have all been entrusted to us.

Apply:

Are you taking care of what has been entrusted to you?

_____

_____

_____

_____

_____

_____

_____

Day Three

Read: 2 Timothy 1:6-14

"For this reason, I remind you to kindle afresh the gift of God which is in you through the laying on of my hands. [7] *For God has not given us a spirit of timidity, but of power and love and discipline.* [8] *Therefore do not be ashamed of the testimony of our Lord or of me His prisoner, but join with me in suffering for the Gospel according to the power of God,* [9] *who saved us and called us with a holy calling, not according to our works, but according to His own purpose and grace, which was granted to us in Christ Jesus from all eternity,* [10] *but has now been revealed by the appearing of our Savior Christ Jesus, who abolished death and brought life and immortality to light through the Gospel,* [11] *for which I was appointed a preacher, an apostle, and a teacher.* [12] *For this reason I also suffer these things, but I am not ashamed, for I know whom I have believed, and I am convinced that He is able to protect what I have entrusted to Him until that day.* [13] *Hold on to the example of sound words that you have heard from me in the faith and love that are in Christ Jesus.* [14] *Protect,*

> *through the Holy Spirit who dwells in us, the treasure which has been entrusted to you."*

Learn: Paul challenged Timothy to mature in his faith by "stirring up" the gift of God in him.

Paul had already acknowledged Timothy's faith and the hand of God on his life. Not only that, he recognized and celebrated the gift of God in Timothy's life. He was saying to his disciple, "I see evidence of God's unique gifting in you. There is a gift of God on your life. That gift had been committed to Timothy (vs. 14). That word is a banking term and carries the idea of a deposit. God made a deposit in your life.

Now ... I want you to stir it up. The image of stirring pictures the stoking of a fire. That doesn't necessarily mean the flame had died; instead, Paul was admonishing Timothy to stoke it into a great flame.

The use of the imperative in vs. 13 is how Timothy will maximize the gift of God in his life. It is by holding tightly to the Word of God that Paul had instilled it in him. Timothy was to hold fast to that pattern.

The way you increase your effectiveness for the cause of Christ and grow more effective at using the gift of

God that He has given to you is through faithful adherence to God's Word.

Paul gave Timothy a pattern. So, any word he advocated, taught, or patterned his life after should follow that same template.

Paul was admonishing Timothy and us, by extension, *"Don't let go of that pattern."* That's the blueprint for your life and ministry and the formula for effective ministry for God's glory.

What gift has God given to you? How can you fan that gift into a flame of faith for His glory?

Apply:

Are you fanning the flame of God's gift in you? What practices do you have in your life to stoke the flame of the fire of faith in you?

_____

_____

_____

_____

_____

_____

Day Four

Read: 2 Timothy 2:1-3

"You therefore, my ^ason, be strong in the grace that is in Christ Jesus. ² The things that you have heard from me in the presence of many witnesses, entrust these to faithful people who will be able to teach others also. ³ Suffer hardship with me, as a good soldier of Christ Jesus."

Learn: Paul exhorted Timothy to mature in his faith by being strong in the grace of God that is in Christ.

How strong is your faith?

Scripture was not written with chapter divisions. Those were added in the early part of the 13th century. Right before Paul gave this charge to Timothy, he had reminded Timothy of a general desertion he had experienced from *"all those in Asia."*

In particular, Paul called out Phygellus and Hermogenes. We are not told what they did, but clearly Paul still felt the sting.

In contrast, however, Paul talked about the refreshing he had received from Onesiphorus and prayed for God's mercy to be on his life. Paul added, *"you know how he ministered to me."* Apparently, that episode was so personal to Paul, he did not even need to recount it.

Paul simply added, *"I'm praying the mercy of the Lord on that man for what he did for me."*

That's when Paul transitioned to a challenge for Timothy. He said, I want you to be strong like Onesiphorus. You've seen those who were weak. I want you to be strong.

Verse 1 is emphatic, *"YOU ... Be strong in grace. "* Paul was calling for confidence and certainty in grace. Grace is Paul's shorthand for expressing how we received from the Lord what we knew we did not deserve.

Be strong in that, not in your accomplishments, but in His. Paul has already recognized the gifts that God gave to Timothy. But he isn't telling Timothy to be confident in his abilities. This isn't a self-help sermon. Paul wanted Timothy to remember God's grace and find his strength in what God did for him.

It is by grace we are saved through faith (Ephesians 2:8–9). I don't have to be strong in my merit. I can be strong in His grace.

Apply:

In what areas do you need to stay strong?

_____

_____

_____

_____

_____

_____

_____

Day Five

Read: 2 Timothy 3:14-15

"You, however, continue in the things you have learned and become convinced of, knowing from whom you have learned them,[15] *and that from childhood you have known the sacred writings, which are able to give you the wisdom that leads to salvation through faith, which is in Christ Jesus."*

Learn: Paul urged Timothy to mature in his faith by continuing in the things he had learned and of which he had been assured.

The idea of the word continue is to stay moving in the same direction. It carries that idea that *"You are on the right track; keep doing that."* It's affirmation and encouragement.

Paul's admonishment to Timothy is to continue in the things he had learned and believed. What you have learned and believed is good. Keep doing that.

In fact, these are things Timothy had learned from childhood. Part of the incentive for continuing is the personal impact of those who invested in him. Timothy knew (just like is probably true for you) that there were people in his life who had been a strong, positive influence on him.

Paul's exhortation to Timothy was—"Don't disappoint them. They established a pattern, a foundation of faith in your life, that was good. Keep doing that."

Paul encouraged Timothy not to abandon what he knew to be true. If he would stay true to the Word of God that was so faithfully implanted in him, it would make him wise and lead him to eternal life through faith in Jesus Christ, who is the focus of the message.

Then, Paul added a reminder. We know His word is true. It is inspired by God and profitable in our lives. But Timothy already knew that. He'd known that since he was a young child. Paul is just reminding him to stay on track.

If you stay true to God's Word, you will be complete and equipped for every good work. If you are in Christ and seeking His will for your life, you are on the right track.

Continue in what you have learned. It will reap an eternal reward.

Apply:

What are areas of your faith you are convinced of and need to continue?

_____

_____

_____

_____

_____

_____

_____

A LIFE DEAR TO GOD

Disciple!

The focus of this last week is on developing believers to become disciple-makers. This is God's desire for every believer. In the providence of God, when a person comes to faith in Christ, the Holy Spirit of God begins a process inside of us.

Jesus talked about this in the parable of the woman mixing leaven in flour (Matthew 13:33). It is one of Jesus' shortest parables but has a rich message about the Kingdom of Heaven. In the parable, the woman is mixing leaven in flour until the leaven is completely mixed together (literally, "hidden") in the flour. At that point, a process has begun that is not immediately evident on the outside until it is finished on the inside.

Jesus is saying that when we come to faith in Him, our lives are hidden in Christ" (cf. Colossians 3:3). The process that has begun in us is intended to ultimately change us completely. The result will be something that transforms us (like leaven rising) completely.

The process takes time. Remember, even Paul said, the process in him wasn't yet complete (Philippians 3:12–14).

If you are a believer in Jesus Christ, the Holy Spirit of God is working inside of you. He is drawing you closer to Himself and attempting to form you into the image of Christ. Then, in a 2 Timothy 2:2 kind of fashion, He uses you to help recreate that same process in others.

Several years ago I was privileged to be asked to write an article for publication on the role of Elders in OT Spiritual awakenings. I entitled my article" Beyond Gerassapience: The Role of Elders in Old Testament Spiritual Awakenings." The title included a wordplay on a book that was edited by Joel A. Ajayi entitled, A Biblical Theology of Gerassapience. In his work, Ajayi clarified that the term "gerassapience" was intended to include aspects of both wisdom and old age. The author does an excellent job of defining wisdom as more than just intelligence, but also skill and even influence. However, the English term, "sapience" does not carry that same nuance.

I was attempting to demonstrate that the role of elders is more than just intellectual, but also influential. As such, I suggested that the terms geraspuissance or gerashegemony would more accurately communicate the potential of influence the elders had through their accumulated wisdom and experience.

Ultimately, I proposed that an even more appropriate term to coin would be "gerashokmah," which would combine the Greek word for old age with the Hebrew term for wisdom with all of its richness.

Here's the great thing about this process. The process doesn't have to be complete in you for you to be used in the lives of others. It is significant that while Paul admitted that God was not yet finished with him, he was still being used by God to disciple others in Christ. God can also use you to do that. So, simultaneous to the Spirit of God working in you, He can use you to help others grow in their faith.

God's goal for you is not just for you to become a disciple. He wants you to be a disciple-maker. Then, in the providence of God, perhaps He will use you to disciple someone who will disciple someone else (and so on). That's God's plan for the kingdom. It's been His plan from the beginning— God working in us and using us to work in the lives of others.

Day One

Read: Acts 20:28

"Be on guard for yourselves and for all the flock, among which the Holy Spirit has made you overseers, to shepherd the church of God, which He purchased with His own blood."

Learn: A disciple-maker is aware of his own needs as well as the needs of those under his care.

Beginning in Acts 20:17, Paul summoned the elders in Ephesus to meet with him and gave them instructions in ministry. He reminded them through his instruction and his example of the importance of service, preaching, teaching, evangelism, discipleship, obedience to the Lord, endurance in their faith, commitment to complete the task assigned to them, importance of godly character, the importance of vigilance in ministry to take care of themselves, to lead the flock, and to care for people, and to refute false teaching.

Acts 20:4 lists a group of people who were with Paul on this journey. Among those was Timothy. It is true that verse 5 says that "these men" went on ahead, but it is unclear if that phrase reflects all of that group who were accompanying Paul or just the final two whose names seem to be set aside from the rest. Note how Paul's use of "we" becomes frequent after verse 4, suggesting that Paul was not alone.

I envision Paul taking Timothy along with him when he met with the leaders of the churches in Ephesus. If so, he would have heard firsthand Paul's admonition to them to *take heed to themselves and to the flock.* That would have been consistent with Paul's development of his young disciple.

Whatever the circumstances, Paul's exhortation to ministry leaders is to care for themselves and for others. Verse 28 reflects Paul's directives that all of the flock should be cared for, the ability to complete the task comes from and through the Holy Spirit, our calling to ministry is a divine appointment, and care of the sheep is critical because Christ sacrificed His life for them.

In ministry, we are not called to titles; we are called to functions! Those of us called into vocational Christian ministry have been established by the Spirit for a specific function in the body. Paul is calling for wisdom, administrative skill, spiritual depth, and physical care of the sheep. Finally, Paul reminded the leaders that Christ purchased the sheep at great cost.

Paul was reminding these leaders to take care of themselves so they could do all of that. Paul was training these disciples to become disciple-makers. That training begins with care.

Apply:

Are you taking care of yourself so that you are able to care for the flock?

_____

_____

_____

_____

_____

_____

_____

Day Two

Read: 1 Timothy 4:1-16

"But the Spirit explicitly says that in later times some will fall away from the faith, paying attention to deceitful spirits and teachings of demons, ² by means of the hypocrisy of liars seared in their own conscience as with a branding iron, ³ who forbid marriage and advocate abstaining from foods that God has created to be gratefully shared in by those who believe and know the truth. ⁴ For everything created by God is good, and nothing is to be rejected if it is received with gratitude; ⁵ for it is sanctified by means of the word of God and prayer. ⁶ In pointing out these things to the brothers and sisters, you will be a good servant of Christ Jesus, constantly nourished on the words of the faith and of the good doctrine which you have been following. ⁷ But stay away from worthless stories that are typical of old women. Rather, discipline yourself for the purpose of godliness; ⁸ for bodily training is just slightly beneficial, but godliness is beneficial for all things since it holds

promise for the present life and also for the life to come. ⁹ It is a trustworthy statement deserving full acceptance. ¹⁰ For it is for this we labor and strive, because we have set our hope on the living God, who is the Savior of all mankind, especially of believers.¹¹Prescribe and teach these things. ¹² Let no one look down on your youthfulness, but rather in speech, conduct, love, faith, and purity, show yourself an example of those who believe. ¹³ Until I come, give your attention to the public reading, to exhortation, and to teaching. ¹⁴ Do not neglect the spiritual gift within you, which was granted to you through words of prophecy with the laying on of hands by the council of elders. ¹⁵ Take pains with these things; be absorbed in them, so that your progress will be evident to all. ¹⁶ Pay close attention to yourself and to the teaching; persevere in these things, for as you do this, you will save both yourself and those who hear you."

Learn: A disciple-maker focuses his ministry and message on the faithful teaching of God's Word.

The conviction that Paul addresses to begin this chapter regards people leaving the faith. It had been revealed to him by the Spirit of God that there will come a day when people abandon their faith. The primary reason that they will do so is because of false teaching. They will believe a lie. The false truths that will dissuade people will come from demonic forces and from evil people. First, they will attack marriage. We are certainly witnessing that assault today. Second, they will make preferences seem pious. Timothy was entrusted to combat false teaching by reminding people of the truth. Truth is the antidote to error.

The effort of the enemy will be to attack God's truth by undermining its impact in the home and in our practice. They will reduce God's inerrant word to preference and silliness. But a faithful servant of the Lord must defend its truth. That's what it means to be a good servant of God.

Faithful disciple-makers must not get caught up in silly arguments that mock God's Word and reduce it to merely a matter of preference and not truth. We stand on and defend God's truth.

Two things stand out in the last part of verse 6. First, the effectiveness of Timothy's *"reminders"* is partially dependent on his living them out. He is to *"carefully follow"* what he teaches others. In other words, we practice what we preach. Second, in doing so, Timothy will be equipped *("nourished")* by the very words he speaks. A disciple-maker lives and receives nourishment from the message he teaches.

We find our health and our hope in the message we deliver.

This is the training program in godliness for a growing disciple. It is our health for today and our hope for eternity. This is why we labor and endure in faith. It is because we know there are eternal matters at stake. The faithful disciple-maker maintains and models a steady diet on the truth of God's Word. That way people both hear it and see it in us.

We must be nourished by and faithfully defend God's Word.

Then Paul emphasized his instructions by employing a series of imperatives:

- 4:11: Command these things ...
- 4:11: Teach these things ...
- 4:12: Be an example ...
- 4:12: Don't let them despise ...
- 4:13: Give attention ...
- 4:14: Do not neglect ...
- 4:15: Meditate ...
- 4:15: Give Attention ...
- 4:16: Take Heed ...
- 4:16: Continue ...

Then, Paul addressed the areas of Timothy's life that should reflect what God is doing in his life. He encouraged Timothy to be an example in word, conduct, love, faith, and purity. That is what you say, what you do, how you relate to people, how you relate to God, and how you live.

Like Timothy, our lives should be a *Demonstration.*

Apply:

In what way are you an example for others?

_____

_____

_____

_____

_____

_____

_____

Day Three

Read: 1 Timothy 1:3

"Just as I urged you upon my departure for Macedonia, to remain on at Ephesus so that you would instruct certain people not to teach strange doctrines."

Learn: A disciple-maker invests the time necessary to disciple others.

While in Thessalonica, Paul sent word to Timothy instructing him to stay in Ephesus, where Paul had sent him. While there, Timothy was to correct false doctrine and rebuke false teachers.

There were things on which Timothy was to focus and others he was to refute. There were things he was to instruct people to pay no attention to and one goal that they were to pursue.

This is a picture of discipleship. Paul was telling Timothy at the front end of his ministry in Ephesus to dig in and stay. One of the first responsibilities in making disciples is committing the time to do it. Disciples are generally developed slowly over time.

Timothy needed to make the message clear and help the people he served understand it. Timothy served as pastor in Ephesus for about three years.

Part of making the message clear is distinguishing it from that which is false. To do that, Paul knew that Timothy would need to correct false doctrine. Paul admonished Timothy that some had departed from faith (1 Timothy 1:6; 6:21; 2 Timothy 2:18) and that others will depart (1 Timothy 4:1; 2 Timothy 4:3-4).

This is precisely what Paul had warned the church in Acts 20:29-30 would happen. Paul even named some of those who had: Hymenaeus and Alexander (1 Timothy 1:20) were *"shipwrecked in their faith,"* and Paul turned them over to Satan; Phygelus and Hermogenes (2 Timothy 1:15) had *"turned away,"* Philetus and Hymenaeus (2 Timothy 2:17) had spread profane and idle babbling like cancer; and Demas (2 Timothy 4:10) had *"forsaken me having loved this world."*

Discipleship is a big task. It requires time, clarity, and defense. Those same functions are needed of us today.

Apply:

Are you willing to commit the Time to Disciple others?

_____

_____

_____

_____

_____

_____

_____

How can you use time strategically to help others grow in their faith?

_____

_____

_____

_____

_____

_____

Day Four

Read: 2 Timothy 2:2

"The things which you have heard from me in the presence of many witnesses, entrust these to faithful people who will be able to teach others also."

Learn: A discipline-maker is careful in choosing those in whom he will invest.

This instruction was at the heart of discipleship. Paul was encouraging Timothy in two ways. First, he was to commit them to others. Second, those to whom he was to commit them are to be faithful. So, he was to pass the message along and also to be careful to whom he entrusted it.

There is both a pattern and a fundamental principle here that we need today in discipleship. The pattern we should follow is exactly as Paul instructed Timothy. The principle is that we need to be careful with God's resources. Jesus instructed His disciples in (Matthew 7:6) not to cast pearls before swine.

Swine representing what was unclean; pearls representing what was pure and valuable. Was Jesus saying, don't preach the Gospel to lost people? Certainly not.

In the previous paragraph Jesus issued the command, *"Judge not lest you be judged."* That's the first sentence of that paragraph, vs. 6 about casting pearls is the last sentence of that paragraph.

Certainly, Jesus was not saying that we should be selective with whom we share the Gospel. But, in one sense, after a person has repeatedly rejected the message, it is appropriate to move on. Jesus isn't saying that we "judge" them to be beasts but so respect the value of our message that we do not allow it to be dishonored.

In another sense, Paul seems to be instructing his disciple to be discerning with whom he entrusts leadership and responsibility of the message. So Timothy was to invest in those who demonstrated a serious commitment to the message.

You and I also have a responsibility with the Word of God. Paul told Timothy to take care of God's word!

Apply:

Do you have someone in your life in whom you are investing?

_____

_____

_____

_____

_____

_____

_____

Day Five

Read: 2 Timothy 4:1-5

"I solemnly exhort you in the presence of God and of Christ Jesus, who is to judge the living and the dead, and by His appearing and His kingdom: ² preach the word; be ready in season and out of season; correct, rebuke, and exhort, with great patience and instruction. ³ For the time will come when they will not tolerate sound doctrine, but wanting to have their ears tickled, they will accumulate for themselves teachers in accordance with their own desires, ⁴ and they will turn their ears away from the truth and will turn aside to myths. ⁵ But as for you, use self-restraint in all things, endure hardship, do the work of an evangelist, and fulfill your ministry."

Learn: A disciple-maker is faithful in sharing the message.

2 Timothy 4 represents the last chapter of Paul's final letter. In all likelihood, these are the final words he wrote. He knew his time was short (2 Timothy 4:6–8), which was the reason for the urgency of his instruction. There were requests that he made of Timothy, but there were also final instructions to Timothy.

Paul's final words of direction to his disciple related to the communication of his faith. He admonished Timothy to be ready, in season and out, to preach the Word. That would involve correction, rebuke, encouragement, patience, and instruction (2 Timothy 3:16-17).

Timothy was to keep getting the message out. Countering the untruth of false teachers was a frequent refrain in Paul's letters to Timothy (1 Timothy 1:6; 6:21; 2 Timothy 2:18; 4:4). In the midst of false teachers, Timothy was to represent the truth. He was the one to clarify what the message says, correct those who live contrary to it, and encourage faithfulness to it.

Timothy was to be a faithful preacher of the Gospel. Not everyone is called to preach, but we are all called to share the message. Paul's urgency not only reflected the nearness of his death but also the importance of the message.

God wants you to be a disciple-maker.

Apply:

How are you sharing your faith?

_____

_____

_____

_____

_____

_____

_____

A LIFE DEAR TO GOD

CONCLUSION

Jesus said, *"Go, therefore, and make disciples of all the nations, baptizing them in the name of the Father and the Son and the Holy Spirit, 20 teaching them to follow all that I commanded you; and behold, I am with you always, to the end of the age."*

Discipleship is about doing. Prayer, Bible Study, Worship, and all the other doings of our faith are all essential to our Christian lives.

Discipleship is also about being. It's about becoming more and more like Christ. It's about a character that is being incrementally conformed to His image. It's about being in His presence with regularity and intentionality.

162

Discipleship is also about going. The imperative of the Great Commission is to make disciples. But incumbent in that process is the assumption of going. That participle, going, carries the imperatival force of the command to make disciples. It is understood. It is expected. We go with a purpose. Discipleship is not accidental. But just going does not produce spiritual maturity.

Discipleship is also about dying. We die to ourselves in order to live for Christ. Jesus said, *"If anyone desires to come after Me, let him deny himself, take up his cross, and follow Me"* (Matthew 16:24). Taking up our cross is about dying. Paul said in Galatians 2:19-20, *"I died ... so I might live."*

Discipleship is all of that. It's doing, being, going, and dying in cooperation with the Spirit of God. It won't happen in an instant. But slowly, incrementally, God is doing something in you.

Discipleship is a journey. The destination is certain, but the path is still being charted. If you have given your heart to Jesus Christ, you are going to end up in heaven. That's already been decided. The admission was purchased at the cross. There's nothing you can do or need to do to impact that final destination. But the route between here and there is seismic.

That's the journey. Your path won't look the same as anyone else's, but God is doing something. Every lesson, every experience, every divinely implanted gift, and every divinely inspired encounter are working together to make you into who God wants you to be.

This study has followed Timothy's life and ministry. But the study isn't about him. It's about you and me. We've been encouraged by his faith and challenged by his faithfulness. Now, the journey is ours. God wants to do a work in your life to grow you into a mature, disciple- making follower of Christ.

Maybe you're not there yet. That's ok.

As you cooperate with the Spirit's guidance in your life to do, be, go, and die as He leads, you'll keep making progress towards the goal of the upward call of Christ Jesus for your life. It's the journey of a lifetime. It's God's plan for you.

That's a Life Dear to God.

Made in the USA
Monee, IL
10 February 2025

11830813R00095